KETO SLOW COOKER COOKBOOK

THE QUICKEST AND EASIEST LOW-CARB KETOGENIC RECIPES TO SHAPE YOUR BODY AND LOSE WEIGHT ON A BUDGET

KATHERINE WALLEN

Additionally, the information in the following pages is intended only for informational purposes and should thus be thought of as universal. As befitting its nature, it is presented without assurance regarding its prolonged validity or interim quality. Trademarks that are mentioned are done without written consent and can in no way be considered an endorsement from the trademark holder.

TABLE OF CONTENTS

Introduction

It is easy to hear people talking about the slow cooker in our days, but what is this appliance that has become famous in kitchens around the world? The slow cooker is nothing more than an electric pot that consumes less energy than traditional gas cooking methods, even the waste of electricity produced by a slow cooker of medium size for the duration of 8 hours and approximately 1700 kWh = comparable to that of a light bulb!

As several of the inventions of the twentieth century, the invention of the slow cooker seems to be credited to the United States of America, from where it spread throughout the world, especially in Europe where this appliance is entering more and more powerfully in the kitchens of families, especially the more numerous and the busier.

How does it work?

It would be really difficult to invent another culinary appliance with practicality and simplicity superior to that of the slow cooker! The most common models simply have a button to turn it on and intensity control, with which you can switch from low to medium or high.

The most advanced models are also called "Multicookers" They have several functions and tools, including an autonomous and adjustable timer, so you can program the shutdown, a function that can be very useful because most of the uses are more than 2 / 3 hours, so it can happen that you are not at home at the time when you need to stop cooking, and your slow cooker will do it automatically.
The main reason why this appliance has become so popular is the practicality. The typical use of the slow cooker is to put all the ingredients inside and let it do everything!

The temperatures at which these appliances operate can usually vary from 100 to 150 degrees. Consider low cooking around 100 degrees and high around 150.

As you can see, these temperatures are much lower than those reached with traditional gas cooking methods, where for some foods (especially meat), temperatures are reached over 250 degrees.

Obviously, cooking times will not be the same, and certainly not the consumption either.
Usually, the food on a slow stove is cooked for durations of time from 2 to 12 hours, depending on what type of food is cooked and the power/size of the slow cooker (there are several models more or less expensive).

The inside walls are made of ceramic, so the food is unlikely to stick thanks to the non-stick properties of this material.
The lid is made of glass so that the user can look inside, even if after the first hours of cooking, the view is dulled because of the steam.

What is Ketogenic Diet?

Ketogenic is a diet that specifically aims to achieve a state of ketosis by decreasing carbohydrates almost entirely, then pushing the organism to feed on ketones.

What are ketones?

Our body needs to draw on sugars to produce energy; if we subject it to a situation of abstinence from them, it replaces them with fats. From this particular type of metabolism, Ketones re produced, from which the famous diet takes its name.

Explained in simpler words, the ketogenic diet is nothing more than a way to push the body to assimilate fat quickly by eliminating carbohydrates, thus simulating a fasting situation for our metabolism.

Although this diet exploded only a few years ago, the concepts inherent in ketonic bodies were already known by doctors of several past generations.

To create this state of ketosis and definitely useful consult your family doctor, as it can be considered an extreme situation and the organism could react in unwanted knots causing thirst, vomiting, nausea, tiredness, stomach pain.

The ketogenic diet therefore involves the consumption of fats and proteins, avoiding complex carbohydrates.
In order to reach easily the state of ketosis we must make our organism believe that we are going through a period of fasting; to do this we will completely eliminate carbohydrates.

However, this does not mean to over-abound with proteins, as the excess ones will be perceived by our organism as sugars. So, we're going to compromise the whole diet plan.

Slow cooker pros and cons

Pros

It is not easy in the twenty-first century, with hectic life rhythms, to maintain a healthy and balanced diet, and the choice to resort to fast food is becoming increasingly frequent.
However, this era, as well as the stress that we are subjected to, offers some advantages, such as technology, technology brought to the kitchen, in this the creation of appliances that can disrupt the world of cooking food, and why not, help you improve your lifestyle!
I have mentioned below some of the advantages of the slow stove that you should definitely take advantage of.

No attention required

The advantage that many people underestimate, I consider the most convenient. It is not gas-powered, therefore no flame and no dangers in general (no gas outlets, defective cylinders, sudden increase of flame, flame extinction, etc. ...) The slow cooker is not connected to the electrical system of the house but is completely independent, and it is connected to the electricity only through the power cord that attaches to the socket.

The alkaline battery models do not have any cable and therefore are completely independent. This means that you can allow putting the food inside the slow cooker, set the timer, close the lid and go out to do the shopping, or go to sleep and leave the whole night cooking without worrying about anything! In the worst case, should there be a malfunction of the appliance, the only risk you will run is that of not having dinner ready!

Practicality

As we have mentioned before, this is the main reason for the success of this appliance. Most of the users are not cooking experts, or they are mothers with three children and a husband working full time, or they are very busy people with very little time available. Anyone can buy a slow cooker cookbook (you even get several for free when you buy the appliance) or look up some recipes online.

Consumption

This advantage has also been mentioned before quite explicitly; I don't think I need to add anything else...

Healthy

We have not yet spoken of the healthy aspects of slow stove cooking. Perhaps we have overlooked the most important point up to now...yes, I say the most important because this method of cooking is very similar to the vapor method. When you close the lid, you implement an airtight closure that does not allow for the escape of steam.

In this way, the nutrients (vitamins, fiber, protein, etc.) of the food are maintained completely during cooking, as opposed to boiling, where a large percentage of them are released into the water.

Tasty

It has been known since middle age that long cooking at low temperatures is the best way to cook any type of food, but the ones that benefit the most are meats, whether white meat, red meat, fish, or game makes no difference.
Not only does slow cooking bring superior tenderness to the meat, but it also creates the ideal conditions for greater absorption of scents and flavors of spices that you put to cook along with the meat.
You just have to try it to believe it...

Washable

The removable parts of the slow cooker (those in contact with the food) are made of litho-ceramic, a particularly non-stick material and therefore easily washable by hand or in the dishwasher, although I suggest not to put them in the washing machine frequently as you will wear the surface layer over time. Even the best quality products wear out in time, more or less depending on the level of maintenance that is applied to them.

Cons

I don't think there will be any particular disadvantages to using a slow cooker, honestly.

-It requires organization and time management because you have to organize your day according to your schedule. If you don't do your calculations well, you risk coming home and finding your dinner not ready, but if you think about it, it's not so impossible to solve mathematical equations ☺.

-Not usable in case you want to make a quick snack!

-Like any other household appliance, there is a slight possibility that it could catch fire and consequently set the house on fire.
To reduce this possibility from minimal to 0, place your slow cooker away from curtains, paper towels, electrical outlets, or under wooden shelves or any other flammable object, especially if you leave it on and go outside or to sleep.

Tips

Never open the slow cooker's lid during cooking because you will disperse the temperature that had accumulated inside and, consequently, lengthen the cooking time.
So always try to put all the ingredients at the beginning (except in some cases).

- Always set the timer to go off an hour before returning home so that you will find a hot dinner, avoiding the risk that it is not ready yet.

- If you intend to cook meat, especially significant cuts, in most cases, it is advisable to let it marinate overnight before cooking.

- Choose cuts of meat with little fat.

- Do not use too much oil or butter.

- If the sauce should be too liquid, you can use a few tablespoons of all-purpose white flour to thicken it.

- As the name suggests, always choose the slowest possible cooking time for your food, so always use low mode.

Turkey

Ham and Cheddar Rolle

SERVE 4   PREPARATION 15m COOKING 4/5h

INGREDIENTS

600 grams of turkey breast
200g spinach
Spoon of butter
50g Parmesan cheese
150g cooked ham
150g cheddar cheese
thyme
2 tablespoons olive oil
100 ml of fruity white wine
Salt and pepper to taste

INSTRUCTIONS

Sauté the spinach in a pan with butter, parmesan
salt, and pepper and set aside.
Take your turkey breast and cut it into 1/2 cm
thick slices (or ask your butcher to slice it for you).
Then spread the slices on a chopping board,
slinging the ends to form a turkey bed. Pour over
the spinach, cover the spinach formed a layer of
ham. Over the ham formed a layer of cheese.
Salt and gently roll it all up, taking care not to
break the balance of the ingredients, then tie
everything with rope.
Insert the separator at the base of the slow cooker
in order to create a detachment, lay your Rolle on
it, pour the white wine over the turkey (drip on the
bottom), and a drizzle of olive oil and thyme.
Cook for at least 4 hours in low mode.

When the Rolle is cooked enough, pull it out of the slow cooker and place it on a chopping board.
Wait a little time for it to cool down a little, cut it into slices and serve it with mashed potatoes!

Rollie Turkey Breast

SERVE 4   PREPARATION   20 M   COOKING 8 H

INGREDIENTS

2 kg of turkey
Fresh Rosemary
Fresh thyme
Salt and grounded black pepper
2 cloves of garlic

INSTRUCTIONS

Prepare our spice mixture by finely chopping the
Rosemary along with the thyme and garlic (you
can also use garlic powder).
Slice your turkey, setting a thickness of ½ inch per
slice, then lay your slices on a cutting board or flat
container and sprinkle them well with the spice
mixture.
Carefully roll up the turkey slices and tie them with
food string, place them inside your slow cooker
creating a gap with the base so as to avoid contact
of the turkey rolls with the hot surface of the slow
stove, and leave to cool for at least 8 hours in low-
temperature mode.
You can serve the turkey some tomato salad or
arugula.

Whole Crispy and Stuffed Turkey

SERVE 10/12   PREPARATION 1h   COOKING 6h

MARINATING INGREDIENTS

1 whole turkey (between 7 to 10 kilos)
3 cloves chopped garlic
salt 300 g
5 medium onions
15 juniper berries
500 ml white wine
Some bay leaf and sage
1 nutmeg
About 300g rosemary and thyme needles
1 spoon of grounded black pepper
Water

FILLING INGREDIENTS

800g bread
milk
200g flour
50 g butter
5 eggs
2 celery stalks
1 onion
1 carrot
100g fresh blueberries
2 tablespoons chopped coriander
chopped sage and thyme 2 tablespoons
1 tablespoon lyophilized garlic
100g chopped nuts
100g chopped almonds
100g pine nuts

200g blue cheese(or gorgonzola)
300 sliced cooked ham
salt and pepper to taste
100 ml olive oil

INSTRUCTIONS

Marinating

Cut the onions, and together with all the
ingredients to be used in the marinade, place them
in a large container plus the whole turkey. With a
coarsely ground pestle, all ingredients, especially
juniper berries.
Pour about a liter of water into the container and
mix well, add the whole turkey, and cover it with
water until it is submerged. Hermetically cover the
container if you can (or use film), place it in the
fridge and leave it to marinate for 2 days.

Filling

Take the bread and soak it in milk for 10 minutes.
Meanwhile, melt the butter in a pan and add the
onions, celery, and chopped carrots, sauté for 5
minutes over light heat. In a container, you will put
the bread soaked in milk, the yolks of 5 eggs, the
sautéed vegetables, the dried fruit, chopped the
herbs and spices. Mix everything with your hands,
add the cheese cut into small pieces, the
blueberries, and dust the flour upstairs and
continue to mix until you form a dough (if you
realize that it is too liquid, add flour or bread).

Slow cooking

Take the turkey that you had marinated for 2 days,
insert the filling inside and tie the paws with rope
so as not to let it out during cooking. You can use a
baking tray at the base of the slow cooker to
create a thickness of 3 centimeters. Put the stuffed
turkey inside and pour over some herb-flavored
butter (simply take a saucepan, melt the butter,
and add your favorite herbs).
Cook for 6 hours (more or less) in low mode. Keep
the heel always damp with a spoon, collect the
butter from the bottom and wet the top of the
turkey. Repeat this process every hour.

Tuna turkey

SERVES 4   PREPARATION 20m   COOKING 6h

INGREDIENTS

1 whole turkey breast
Veggie mix (carrot, celery, and onion)
50 ml olive oil
1/2 poor glass of rosé wine
Veg stock
Fresh thyme
1 teaspoon lyophilized garlic
1 bay leaf
Salt and pepper to taste

For the tuna sauce

1 can of tuna (preferably in olive oil)
1 shot of Brandy
Fresh coriander
8 anchovies
2 eggs
About ten Capers
5 cherry tomatoes
Salt and pepper to taste

INSTRUCTIONS

Start chopping the vegetables (1 celery, 1 carrot, and 1 onion) and place them at the bottom. Pour a tablespoon of olive oil, then lay the entire turkey breast on the vegetables, pour in the wine, bay leaves, fresh thyme, icy garlic, and salt and pepper to taste.

Cook for 6 hours in low mode. After about 2 hours of cooking, add a few tablespoons of vegetable broth.
After about 6 hours, check that the turkey is cooked enough inside. Then slice it and serve it sprinkled with Tuna sauce!

Tuna sauce

Boil the eggs until they become boiled, wait for them to cool a little, shell them, and put them in a blender. Add the anchovies, a shot of brandy, the cherry tomatoes, the capers, the coriander, a sprinkle of salt and pepper, the tuna, and finally, the olive oil.
Blend for about a minute, and your delicious Tuna sauce is ready!

Thanks Giving's Day Turkey

SERVE 8/10 PREPARATION 30 m   COOKING 8h

INGREDIENTS

Whole Turkey
1 veg stock cube
300ml rose wine
Salt and black pepper to taste
300g Butter
2 sprigs of Rosemary
Marinating
2 spoons of salt
1 glass of apple vinegar
water
For the gravy
1 small onion
1 spoon olive oil
3 tablespoons of flour
150 ml full-body red wine
150 ml beef stock

INSTRUCTIONS

Put the turkey inside a large container or hermetic bag. Pour in the apple cider vinegar, salt, and cover with water. Leave to marinate for at least 48 hours for the great success of this dish.
After marinating, it prepares the whole turkey for cooking.
Then place the appropriate baking tray inside the slow cooker to create a thickness from the bottom, and lay the turkey on it, pour the wine, and turn on the slow cooker.

Cook for about 1 hour in low mode, then add about 200ml of vegetable broth and leave to cook for another 3 hours and add some butter and Rosemary. Cook for another 4 hours by interspersing every 30 minutes to collect liquids from the bottom and spray the turkey to remain juicy.

In total, the turkey should take around 8 hours of cooking in total. But remember that at a lower temperature you make it sew and better and the result.

When you think it is ready, stick it and serve it with roast potatoes and gravy sauce on top!

Gravy Sauce

It is easy to go to the store and buy the gravy sauce ready, but it's even easier to make it at home!

Take a very finely chopped onion (small) and sauté it in a saucepan with olive oil, add the broth, wine and bring to a boil.

Lower the heat and add the flour little by little, turning the sauce to prevent lumps from accumulating. Continue until you reach the desired consistency.

Bacon and cheesy Turkey

SERVE 4   PREPARATION 10m   COOKING 6h

INGREDIENTS

1 whole turkey breast
100ml extra virgin olive oil
300ml veg stock
15 slices of bacon
Black pepper to taste
Cheese sauce
1 spoon olive oil
1 clove garlic
Chopped coriander
200ml cream
200g cheddar
200g blue cheese
100g parmesan cheese

INSTRUCTIONS

Wet the surfaces of the turkey breast with oil and
sprinkle them with black pepper powder, then roll
the bacon slices around it as if to form a second
skin.
With food, twine forms a cobweb that wraps the
entire chest so as not to slide away from the slices
of bacon.
Then insert everything into the slow cooker,
making sure to create a detachment from the
bottom.
Pour the vegetable broth over the bottom and start
the slow cooker in low mode for 6 hours. Wet the
turkey frequently by pouring over the liquids that
you will curl from the bottom with a spoon.

Make sure your chest is cooked at the right spot,
then pull it out of the slow cooker, slice it and
serve it with a side dish of roast potatoes and
cheese sauce everywhere!
Cheese sauce
Much simpler than it looks...Take a saucepan, pour
a tablespoon of oil and sauté a very fine chopped
clove of garlic for 30 seconds, then add the cream
(all over low heat).
Mix well. As soon as the first bubbles pop up, add
the cheddar and blue cheese cut into cubes. Mix
until the cheese melts completely, then add the
grated parmesan and chopped coriander.
Turn off the heat and continue to mix the sauce
until the parmesan melts completely.
Your creamy cheese sauce is ready!

Turkey rollies

SERVES 4   PREPARATION 20M   COOKING 6H

INGREDIENTS

12 slices of turkey breast
1 teaspoon lyophilized garlic
2 tablespoons extra virgin olive oil
300g ham
200g grated Parmesan cheese
2 eggs
4 panini
Veggie mix (carrots, onion, celery)
milk
coriander
1 teaspoon dried oregano
Salt and pepper to taste
10 potatoes

INSTRUCTIONS

First, prepare the filling. Then put the mixture of veggie in a saucepan, 1 carrot and onion, and a stalk of celery (all chopped) with a tablespoon of olive oil. Simmer for 10 minutes and set aside. Soak the bread in a container with milk, leave them there for 5 minutes so that they will absorb as much milk as possible, and squeeze them. Take a container where you will mix the dough. Then put in the bread soaked in milk, the sauté of vegetables, break 2 eggs inside, add the grated Parmesan cheese, and finally, the ham cut into thin strips.

Add the spices, then sprinkle over a teaspoon of lyophilized garlic, chopped coriander, and a sprinkle of salt and pepper. Mix everything carefully and place it in the fridge for a half-straight covered with cling film.
Take your turkey slices, and with a rolling pin, try to extend them as much as you can, then insert the filling inside and roll.
You can hold them still with a stick or with a food rope.
Cut the potatoes as you like and place them on the bottom of the slow cooker. We're going to use them as low.
Then pour half a glass of water over them and lay the turkey rolls upstairs.
Switch on the slow cooker and cook for 6 hours in low mode.
Your simple and delicious rolls are ready!

Polynesian turkey thighs

SERVE 4   PREPARATION 5m   COOKING 6h

INGREDIENTS

4 turkey thighs
10 sweet potatoes
200 g coconut milk
1 onion
2 carrots
 2 ginger roots
Fresh chilly
Juice of 2 limes
1 spoon of Chopped parsley
cloves
some bay leaf
peanut oil
2 tablespoons extra virgin olive oil
Salt and black pepper to taste

INSTRUCTIONS

This is a delicious recipe, much easier to prepare than it seems...
You just have to put all the ingredients inside the slow cooker and let it do time...
So let's start with vegetables. Finely chop the onion, cut the carrots and potatoes into small pieces and place them at the base of the slow cooker.
Lay the turkey thighs upstairs, then the rest of the ingredients.
Switch on the slow cooker and cook for 6 hours in low mode.

Your thighs are ready. Serve on a bed of basmati rice!

Orange Turkey

SERVE 4   PREPARATION 10m   COOKING 6h

INGREDIENTS

1 whole turkey breast
Mixed herbs (sage, thyme, Rosemary)
1 onion
60g almonds
4 oranges
flour
1 tablespoon extra-virgin olive oil
salt and white pepper to taste

INSTRUCTIONS

Such an easy recipe. Finely chop the onion and put
it at the base of the slow cooker. Also, add the
almonds and lay the entire turkey breast on them.

Squeeze the 4 oranges and pour the juice inside the slow cooker. Turn on and cook for 4 hours in low mode.
Pull the chest out of the slow cooker and slice it, put the slices back inside, sprinkle the flour on the meat, add salt, white pepper, and the mixture of herbs and cook for another 2 hours.
Your orange turkey with almonds and ready, garnish with orange washers!

Ginger Oily Turkey

SERVE 4   PREPARATION 10m   COOKING 6h

INGREDIENTS

Whole turkey(or Chicken) breast
200 ml extra virgin olive oil
100 ml fruity white wine
2 medium ginger roots
1 small onion
1 clove of garlic
1 sprig of Rosemary
salt and white pepper to taste

INSTRUCTIONS

Gently crush the garlic clove in order to extract the juices while remaining whole (so easily removable) and place it inside the slow cooker.
Chop the onion very finely and add it together with the oil and wine inside the slow cooker.
Cut the breast into small pieces (I recommend cutting it into slices initially and then into shreds) and add it to the slow cooker along with the ginger roots cut into 2 and the rest of the ingredients.
Start the slow stove on low mode and cook for 6 hours.
Remove the garlic clove and ginger and serve on a bed of toasted bread.
Enjoy!

Turkey thighs with wine and potatoes

SERVE 4   PREPARATION 10m   COOKING 6h

INGREDIENTS

4 turkey thighs
10 potatoes
Mixed herbs (Sage, Rosemary, thyme)
1 glass of white wine
1 glass of red wine
Salt and pepper to taste
A few tablespoons of olive oil

INSTRUCTIONS

Take a pan from the thick bottom, put it on the fire, add some olive oil and let the chicken thighs burn evenly to create a crust that retains liquids internally, for 30 minutes more or less. Blend with white wine for another 10 minutes and remove your thighs from the heat.
Cut the potatoes into tiny pieces and put them on the bottom of the slow cooker. Pour the red wine on them, the herbs, olive oil.
Lay the pre-cooked turkey thighs on the potatoes and cook for at least 5 hours in medium/low mode.
Dish it's ready!

Lamb

Slow minty lamb

SERVE 4 PREPARATION 15m COOKING 8h

INGREDIENTS

500g sweet potatoes
4 carrots
2 celery sticks
Fresh chilly
salt and black pepper to taste
1 small boneless lamb shoulder
2 lamb stock cubes
200g mint sauce
Fresh mint as garnish

INSTRUCTIONS

-Wash the potatoes and cut them into pieces not too small, and above all, do not remove the skin and put them in the slow cooker.
-repeat the same operation with the celery.
-Wash the carrots, remove the skin, cut them into small pieces and put them in the slow cooker on top of the potatoes, and add the chopped fresh chilly
- Place the lamb on top of the vegetables and add salt and pepper.
-Add the broth and mint sauce and simmer for at least 8 hours.

Winy lamb shoulder

SERVE 4   PREPARATION   20m COOKING 8h

INGREDIENTS

- 1kg lamb shoulder joint
- 2 cubes of meat stock
- 200 ml red wine
- Selection of your favorite aromatic herbs
- Salt and black pepper to taste
- 1 teaspoon corn flour
- 1 teaspoon berry jelly

INSTRUCTIONS

-Gently place all ingredients except cornmeal and gelatin in slow cooker.
-Set a low intensity, cover, and let cook for at least 7 hours.
-Open the lid take out the lamb, debone it, and put it back in the pan.
-Add the corn flour, mix well and leave to cook for another half an hour.
-Take out the meat definitively, cut it into portions, and plate it.
-Add the gelatin to the sauce and pour it over the meat.
The dish is served!

Marinated lamb

SERVE 4   PREPARATION 15m COOKING 6h

INGREDIENTS

2 lamb shank
2 extra virgin olive spoons
1 lemon
The mix of your favorite's aromatic herbs (mint, oregano, thyme)
1 bay leaf
1 clove of garlic
Cloves
Lamb stock
salt and pepper to taste

INSTRUCTIONS

To reach the maximum concentration of flavors, let your 2 lamb shanks marinate for a couple of hours. Then we take an airtight food bag (if you do not have a large enough bag, you can use a baking tray and then cover it with film), we insert inside the 2 lamb shanks, the aromatic herbs, the bay leaf, the cloves, the salt the pepper and the juice of a lemon. Close the bag well so that it does not pass air and place it in the fridge for at least 2 hours.

Prepare a saucepan with boiling water where you will melt the cube of broth. If you have bones or lamb remains, put them to boil together with the broth. They will transfer an additional flavor.

Pour the contents of the marinade into the slow cooker, add 2 ladles of broth (do not completely cover the lamb), and start your slow cooker in low mode for at least 6 hours.
Your lamb shanks are ready!

Saddle and lamb loins with potatoes

SERVE 4   PREPARATION 10m   COOKING 6h

INGREDIENTS

Saddle and lamb loins
1 spoon of extra virgin olive oil
15 baby potatoes
1 teaspoon lyophilized garlic (or a finely chopped clove)
1 lemon1 onion
Mixed your favorite herbs (rosemary, thyme, mint, or oregano)
2 bay leaves
1 glass Water
1 glass of wine
Spices (black pepper, juniper, cloves)
Salt to taste

INSTRUCTIONS

Again, I strongly suggest leaving the lamb to marinate for a couple of hours.
Then place the pieces of lamb with wine, spices, garlic, and lemon juice in an airtight bag, close it and store it in your fridge for 2 hours.
Clean the potatoes well. You do not have to peel them necessarily. In fact, I prefer them with the peel.

Cut them in half and put them at the base of the slow cooker to form a bed.

Salt the potatoes, add a glass of water to the bottom of the slow cooker, and the entire contents of the bag you had put to marinate. Add the bay leaves, chopped onion, and start the slow cooker for 6 hours in low mode.
Your lamb with potatoes is ready to delight you and your guests!

Lamb pate

SERVE 4   PREPARATION 10   COOKING 6h

INGREDIENTS

200 g of internal organs (liver or heart or lungs)
80ml brandy (the cheapest one you have at home)
Vinegar
2 tablespoons olive oil
100 g butter
1 onion
1 carrot
1 celery stick
2 tomatoes
1 clove of garlic
2 bay leaves
200 ml broth
Salt and black pepper to taste

INSTRUCTIONS

Put the entrails to marinate in an airtight bag with
vinegar for 2 hours.
Prepare a pot where you will sauté with olive oil
and onion finely chopped together with the carrot,
tomatoes, and celery, also finely chopped.
Add the entrails to the sauté and let cook for 5
minutes over low heat.
Pour your sauté into the slow cooker, add a
coarsely cut clove of garlic and the rest of the
ingredients.
Let cook for 5 hours over low heat.
Taste, and if you think the meat needs another
hour of cooking, let go of another hour.

Pour the contents into a baking tray and let cool. Remove the bay leaves and when it is cold enough, blend everything.
Your lamb pate is ready to be enjoyed on toasted pieces of bread!

Lamb entrails

SERVE 4   PREPARATION 10m   COOKING 6h

INGREDIENTS

600 g internal organs of lamb
White wine vinegar
1 tablespoon oil
100g green olive groves
1 clove of garlic
1/2 onion
200 g tomato sauce
Coriander, 19
150 ml full-bodied red wine
Salt and black pepper to taste

INSTRUCTIONS

Particularly important to put to marinate with
vinegar the entrails of the lamb for at least 2 hours
to eliminate any smell.
After that, you ski the meats well under cold water.
Chop the onion and sauté it in a pan with olive oil
and a pounded clove of garlic and olive groves.
Add the lamb and simmer for a few minutes.
Transfer everything inside the slow cooker, add the
wine and tomato sauce, and cook for 6 hours in
low mode.
Serve the entrails on a loaf of toasted bread with a
little butter and decorate with chopped coriander!

Agnello alla Sardignola

SERVE 4   PREPARATION 10m   COOKING 6h

INGREDIENTS

700g pieces of lamb
2 tablespoons olive oil
1/2 kilo artichoke hearts
1 glass of fruity white wine
2 cloves of garlic
Salt and pepper to taste

INSTRUCTIONS

A very simple recipe to prepare and super tasty!
Take the pieces of lamb and let them burn in a
red-hot pan. Turn them every 5 minutes to create
a uniform outer crust that will hold the meat juices
inside to keep it juicy.
Cut the garlic very finely and put it to heat with a
little oil at low temperature inside a pot, add the
artichokes already clean (get only the hearts) and
the wine, cook for 7 minutes over low heat, and
transfer everything inside the slow cooker, add the
lamb the salt and black pepper and cook for 6
hours in low mode.
Your delicious lamb is ready!

Porcini Lamb

SERVE 4   PREPARATION 15m   COOKING 6h

INGREDIENTS

4 pieces of Lamb
300 g porcini mushrooms
1 glass of dry white wine
some laurel leaves
2 cloves Garlic
A few cloves
50 ml lemon juice
1 tablespoon extra-virgin olive oil
Salt, thyme, and black pepper to taste

INSTRUCTIONS

Cut the pieces of lamb into small cubes and put
them to marinate in a hermetic food bag with
thyme, lemon juice, and chopped garlic and wine
for about an hour.
Meanwhile, sauté the mushrooms with olive oil.
Transfer the mushrooms to the slow cooker
forming a uniform base on the bottom.
Add the contents of the bag to the slow cooker
along with the rest of the ingredients and cook for
6 hours in low fashion.
The dish is ready!
You can serve it with a side dish of roast potatoes!

Shepherd's lamb

SERVE 4   PREPARATION 15m   COOKING 6h

INGREDIENTS

4 lamb steaks
Thyme and rosemary just enough
flour just enough
2 tablespoons olive oil
2 cloves of garlic
2 anchovies
1 spoon of Butter
100g green olive groves
50g cappers
50g pine nuts
Apple cider vinegar just enough
Salt and pepper to taste

INSTRUCTIONS

Cut your steaks into small pieces and flour them
well, perhaps oiling them first so that the flour
adheres better.
Pour the cider vinegar into the slow cooker along
with the butter, olives, capers, and pine nuts, add
the floured pieces of lamb and start the slow
cooker in low mode.
After 2 hours, add the chopped garlic, rosemary,
and thyme;
After 5 hours, add the anchovies the salt, and
black pepper;
Cook for another hour, and your lamb is ready!

Slow Agrodolce Lamb

SERVE 4   PREPARATION 10m   COOKING 4h

INGREDIENTS

4 pezzi di spalla d'agnello
2 cipolle piccole
3 cucchiai di olio d'oliva
300g salsa di pomodoro
100ml aceto balsamico
2 cucchiai di zucchero di canna

qualche foglia di basilico
Qualche chiodo di garofano
Salt and black pepper to taste

INSTRUCTIONS

Pierce the onions and sauté them with olive oil and
tomato sauce in a pan.
Add the pieces of lamb, vinegar and let fade for 5
minutes over high heat.
Transfer everything inside the slow cooker, add the
spices and cook in low mode for 3 hours.
Add 1/2 glass of water, the brown sugar, basil, and
spices cook for another hour.
Your sweet and sour lamb is ready!

Pork

Chunk Shank

SERVE 4   PREPARATION 30m   COOKING 6h

INGREDIENTS

1 pork shank
50g butter
1 spoon olive oil
the mixture of your favorite spices
3 cloves of minced garlic (or 2 teaspoons of freeze-
dried garlic)
200g white potatoes
200g sweet potatoes
1 leek
100g white olives
200ml beef stock
200 ml fruity white wine (or what you have opened
at home)
Salt to taste

INSTRUCTIONS

For the best results, I suggest that you first sear
the shank. Then take a frying pan with a thick
bottom, large enough to hold the shank both
lengthwise and widthwise, and heat it well. Add
some olive oil. When it is boiling hot, place the
shank in the pan and turn it frequently (about 5
minutes per side) in order to create a uniform
outer crust. Proceeding in this way will prevent the
internal juices from leaking out, so the meat inside
will be incredibly tender and juicy!

Turn your appliance on low and pour in the butter, thinly sliced leek, garlic, olives, white wine, and stock.
Sprinkle the shank with your spices (except for the salt) and pour in the butter.
When the butter has melted, place the shank in the slow cooker.
Cook for 2 hours, after which add your potato mix to the inside of the slow stove and cook on low for another 4 hours.
Your soft, juicy, and delicious shank with potatoes is ready!

Pork trimmings and sausage with sauce

SERVES 4 PREPARATION 20M COOKING 8H

INGREDIENTS

400g of pork trimmings
300 g pork sausage
50 ml fruity white wine
Veg mix(1 onion1 carrot1 celery stalk chopped)
1 garlic clove
1-liter tomato sauce
10 small wine grapes tomatoes
2 tablespoons of extra virgin olive oil
Salt and black pepper to taste

INSTRUCTIONS

Let's start by preparing our veg mix, then chop a carrot, an onion, and a stick of celery and sauté for 5 minutes over low heat with a tablespoon of olive oil (we recommend using a large pot because we will add the meat later) add the pork and increase the heat slightly and let everything brown together for another 5 minutes, then add the wine, increase the heat a little more and let everything brown for another 5 minutes.
Then we transfer everything into our slow cooker and add the rest of the ingredients (chopped garlic or whole so you can remove it if not desired, and tomatoes cut in half).
Let it cook on slow mode for at least 8 hours.

You can serve the dish on top of toasted garlic bread or roasted potatoes; you can also use the sauce for pasta!

Pork Tasty Choppy

SERVE 6   PREPARATION 20 m   COOKING 6 h

INGREDIENTS

·   6 medium size bone-in pork chops—
preferably blade, shoulder, or sirloin chops;
·   500 ml of water
·   Selection of your favorite spices
·   2 chopped onions
·   4 chopped carrots
·   4 chopped potatoes
·   1 Chopped fennel bulb
·   1 chopped Apple
·   Little box of barry(preferably Rasberry)
·   1 apple cider
·   Salt and black pepper to taste

INSTRUCTIONS

-For an excellent result of the dish is advisable to
leave the chops at low temperature completely
submerged in water and salt for at least 2 hours.
-After that, dry the chops with paper towels and
sear them in a pan with the chopped onions (do
not cook for more than 1 minute per side), season
both sides with salt and black pepper.
- place the chops in the slow cooker along with the
rest of the ingredients (cut into small pieces)
- leave to cook for an average of 6 hours, then
debone the chops and serve by pouring the juice
and vegetables over them.

Il Polpettone della nonna

SERVE 4   PREPARATION 1 h   COOKING 6 h

INGREDIENTS

700 of mixed minced meat (veal and pork)
200 grams of pork sausage
200 g of bread
400 ml of milk
2 eggs
400g of parmesan cheese
Breadcrumbs to taste
Salt and black pepper to taste
2 garlic cloves
200 g parsley
nutmeg to taste

INSTRUCTIONS

Get a large enough container for all the
ingredients, or find a marble, plastic, or metal
surface where you can work.
First, cut the bread into small slices and dip them
into the milk. Leave them 10 minutes to absorb the
milk completely.
Separately organize all the ingredients you need,
then finely chop the garlic and parsley. Add them
to the meat mixture along with the grated
parmesan, salt pepper, and grated nutmeg and
finally the milk with the soaked bread.
Mix the mixture with your hands for a few minutes
and wrap it in multiple layers of film, giving it an
elongated shape (like a suppository), after which
leave it in the fridge for half an hour.

Remove it from the fridge, remove the foil and place it in the center of the slow cooker avoiding contact with the bottom (use a metal base to hold it up, creating a gap of a few centimeters).
Set the slow cooker for 6 hours at low mode, and that's it!

Le Polpette della Nonna

SERVE 4   PREPARATION 30m   COOKING 5h

INGREDIENTS

500g of ground beef
500 g of sausage
200g of milk
300g bread
2 cloves garlic, minced
half a small onion finely chopped
1 teaspoon freshly ground pepper
1 teaspoon dried oregano
100g grated Parmesan cheese
2 eggs
parsley, salt, and pepper to taste

The sauce

1 kg of tomato sauce

1 of medium onion finely chopped
2 bay leaf
Salt and black pepper to taste
pinch of sugar (to correct the acidity)

INSTRUCTIONS

Let's start by preparing the sauce.
Chop the garlic and fry it on a low flame for a few
seconds with olive oil (Do not burn it), then pour
the tomato sauce and let it cook for 10 minutes on
a low flame. Then add salt, pepper, and sugar, mix
it, taste it, and if you think it is necessary, add a
little more salt without exaggerating.

Grandma's Meatballs

Get a container large enough for all the
ingredients, or find a marble, plastic, or metal
surface where you can work.
First, cut the bread into small slices and dip them
in the milk. Leave them 10 minutes to fully absorb
the milk.
Organize separately all the ingredients you need,
then finely chop the garlic and parsley and add
them to the meat mixture along with grated
Parmesan cheese, salt, and pepper, finally, the
milk with the soaked bread.
Mix the mixture with your hands for a few minutes,
then with the help of a scale, divide it into many
small meatballs of about 150/200 grams each.

Cooking

Turn on the oven to 150 degrees and cook the
meatballs in a tray for 10 minutes so that they
release the fat.
Pour the sauce inside your slow cooker, then add
the meatballs that you have previously degreased
and let them cook for five hours on low heat.
Ready!

Pork loin in sweet and sour sauce

SERVE 4   PREPARATION 20m   COOKING 6h

INGREDIENTS

1 kg of pork loin
salt and pepper to taste
1 garlic clove
3 tablespoons of sugar
3 tablespoons balsamic vinegar
1 tablespoon corn-starch
 2 tablespoons soy sauce

INSTRUCTIONS

Finely mince the garlic, pour it into a small
container and add salt and pepper, mix them with
a teaspoon. Sprinkle the loin slices evenly with this
mixture and cook on the slow stove for about 5
hours, do not forget to add a thin layer of water to
the bottom of the slow cooker.
Separately, take a small saucepan, heat it and add
the balsamic vinegar initially and all the other
ingredients to follow. Let it cook on low mode for
10 minutes, turning it frequently; you should get a
medium density.
Take the pork loin slices that you have cooked for
5 hours on the slow stove and sprinkle with the
glaze. Place them in the oven and brown them for
15 minutes.

Cherry Porky

SERVE 4   PREPARATIONS 20m   COOKING 6h

INGREDIENTS

1kg of pork loin
 400g of cherries
Flour, butter, and salt to taste

INSTRUCTIONS

Let the butter melting in a small pan and add the
salt and flour, stir until medium thick.
Sprinkle the pork loin slices with butter, flour, and
salt and place them on top of a layer of cherries
(the cherries must be pitted and crushed coarsely)
that you had previously created on the bottom of
the slow cooker in order to create a detachment
with the bottom. Repeat the operation several
times until you run out of meat, so you will have
several layers of meat and cherries.
Pour the cream of butter and flour that you created
earlier into the slow stove and cook on low for 6
hours.

White Bolognese

SERVE 4   PREPARATION 10m   COOKING 4h

INGREDIENTS

1kg of sausage
700 g of zucchini
700g of carrots
300g of almonds
100ml dry white wine
1 spoon of extra virgin olive oil
1 large onion
Salt and pepper to taste

INSTRUCTIONS

Cut the onion very fine, and let it fry with a
tablespoon of extra virgin olive oil. Cut the zucchini
and carrots and add them to the fry.
Do not cook for more than 10 minutes.
Pour your sautéed vegetables into the slow cooker
along with the rest of the ingredients and cook for
4 hours on low mode.
Your white Bolognese is ready!
It goes great with mashed or roasted potatoes.

Asian pork strips

SERVE 4   PREPARATION 10m   COOKING 4h

INGREDIENTS

800 g of pork slices
150 g of almonds
3 small leeks
80 ml soy sauce
400 ml of water
200g flour
Salt and pepper to taste

INSTRUCTIONS

First, take the almonds, peel them and cook them
in the oven for 30 minutes.
While the almonds are cooking, cut the pork into
small pieces (about a cubic inch each) and sprinkle
them evenly with flour.
When the almonds are done, pour all the
ingredients into the slow stove (we recommend not
to exaggerate with salt because soy sauce contains
ga a good amount of it) and cook for 4 hours on
low mode.
The dish is ready!
Serve it with a side of sweet roasted potatoes or a
salad.

Pork loin with apples

SERVE 4   PREPARATION   5m   COOKING   6h

INGREDIENTS

1 whole pork loin
4 potatoes
1 apple
2 cinnamon sticks
salt and white pepper to taste

INSTRUCTIONS

A simple recipe and, at the same time, very tasty.
Cut the potatoes into large pieces and place them
in the bottom of the slow cooker to form a bed.
Take your apple and cut it into 8 equal slices.
Take the whole loin and make cuts on the surface
large enough to fit the apple slices. Try to keep an
even spacing to cover the entire surface of the loin.
Then lay the loin on top of the potatoes, add salt
and white pepper and cinnamon sticks, and cook
for at least 6 hours.
That is it!

Healthy Pork chops

SERVE 4   PREPARATION 5M   COOKING 6H

INGREDIENTS

4 pork chops (200g each)
1 glass of white wine
1 carrot
1 onion
1 celery stalk
1 sprig of rosemary
1 clove of garlic
2 bay leaves
200ml vegetable broth
Salt and pepper to taste

INSTRUCTIONS

Chop the onion, carrot, and celery and sauté with a tablespoon of olive oil.

Transfer the sauté into the slow cooker and lay the pork chops on top of that (you can choose to sear the chops so as to create a crust, before putting them inside the slow cooker), pour the glass of white wine, herbs, and broth, 1 teaspoon of salt, a whole garlic clove(so you can remove it easily after cooking)a sprinkled of black pepper and cook for 6 hours in low mode.
Serve the chops with a side dish of mashed potatoes.

Asparagus chops

SERVES 4 PREPARATION 10M COOKING 6H

INGREDIENTS

4 pork chops of 250g each
100g fresh porcini mushrooms
200 g asparagus
1/2 glass of white wine
2 tablespoons margarine(or butter)
 3 tablespoons extra virgin olive oil
1 clove of garlic
2 tablespoons flour
1 white onion
Salt and pepper to taste

INSTRUCTIONS

Take a pan with the bottom, often bring it to
temperature and let the chops burn 5 minutes per
side.
Cut the fresh mushrooms coarsely, the asparagus,
into pieces of about 2 centimeters and put them on
the bottom of the slow cooker. Lay the pork chops
over the vegetables, add a sprinkling of flour on
the meat, a chopped onion, a whole clove of garlic
(lightly crush the garlic clove so that the juices
come out, keeping it whole) so you can easily
remove it at the end of cooking.
Close the lid of the slow cooker. Let it cook for 6
hours in low mode.
Add salt and pepper and serve.

Fish

Slow Fresh Water

SERVE 6   PREPARATION 10 m   COOKING 1 h

INGREDIENTS

- 6 boneless salmons fillets
- 1 glass of water
- 1 glass fruity white wine
- The juice of 1 lemon
- 1 shallot, thinly sliced
- Some bay leaf
- Chopped coriander or any preference herbs
- Salt and black pepper to taste

INSTRUCTIONS

Gently place the salmon in the slow cooker (we recommend placing the skin side in contact with the pan).
Add all the other ingredients gently and let it simmer for at least 50 minutes.
Check after that more or less how cooked the salmon is. If you think it is ready, do not cook it further, or you will risk drying out the meat.
The dish is ready. You can serve it with roasted potatoes or steamed asparagus.

Stewed codfish with potatoes and olives

SERVE 2   PREPARATION   15 M COOKING 5 H

INGREDIENT

½ kilo of codfish
½ kilo of potatoes
150 g pitted black olives
1 white onion
2/3 bay leaves
2 tablespoons of extra virgin olive oil
Salt and black pepper to taste

INSTRUCTIONS

Wash the potatoes and cut them into rounds trying to keep the same size for each cut so that they cook evenly, leave them with their skins on if you prefer.
Place the sliced potatoes in a bowl and mix them with the thinly sliced onions, salt and pepper and pour half of the contents into your slow cooker to create a base on which to place the fish, add a drizzle of olive oil and cover with the rest of the potatoes.
Turn on your slow cooker and set it to a medium mode for at least 5 hours.

Salmon in a slow cooker

SERVE 4   PREPARATION 10m   COOKING 4h

INGREDIENTS

4 salmon fillets
veggie mix (potato, broccoli, asparagus)
1 tablespoon of extra virgin olive oil
Salt and pepper to taste

INSTRUCTIONS

Another simple and tasty recipe to prepare in the morning for breakfast and have ready for lunch or even before!

Simply clean and cut the vegetables into small pieces and place them in the bottom of the slow cooker to form a bed.
Lightly salt the vegetables and start the slow cooker on low. Add a tablespoon of olive oil and place the salmon fillets on top of the vegetables. Let it cook for 4 hours.
Add black pepper evenly, both on the fish and vegetables, and serve!

Giltheads bream with potatoes

SERVE 2   PREPARATION 10m   COOKING 4h

INGREDIENTS

- 2 giltheads
- 4 potatoes
- 1 garlic clove
- Mixed herbs
- (we recommend rosemary, thyme, fresh oregano, or basil)
- 50 ml dry white wine
- 1 tablespoon olive oil
- Salt and pepper to taste

INSTRUCTIONS

If you are not very familiar with cleaning fish, we recommend that you ask the fishmonger to clean it for you.
If you cannot buy it already cleaned, don't worry! It is not difficult.
Cut off the fins of the gilthead with a knife or scissors, remove all scales, make a long cut under the belly of the fish, all the way down the fish (from the thing to the head) and remove the internal organs. Rinse the fish under cold water and they are ready to be dressed.
Then insert inside the fish your chopped herbs along with garlic and some lemon juice.
Cut the potatoes into very thin rounds and place them on the bottom of the slow cooker forming a bed on which you will place the fish.

Season the potatoes with salt and pepper, add a
drizzle of oil and the wine and finally place the
gilthead bream on top of the potatoes.
Turn on your slow stove and cook for 4 hours on
low mode.

Bon Appetit!

Swordfish rolls

SERVE 4   PREPARATION 30m   COOKING 4h

INGREDIENTS

3oo g swordfish
Basil 8 leaves
Cherry tomatoes
4 big tomatoes
100 ml fruity white wine
fresh chilly
1 teaspoon freeze-dried garlic
Basil and green olives to taste
Breadcrumbs
1 tablespoon olive oil
Salt and pepper to taste

INSTRUCTIONS

Let's start with the filling.
Slide the tomatoes into very small pieces (as if you
were making a bruschetta), add the breadcrumbs,
salt and pepper, garlic and basil, pour a drizzle of
olive oil, and mix well.
Let your filling rest in the fridge for half an hour so
that the ingredients thicken with flavors and
fragrances between them.
For a perfect outcome of this dish, the thickness of
the pada fish slices is fundamental, about 1/2
centimeter. Simply tell your trusted fishmonger
that you need the swordfish cut for rolls, he should
know how to cut it so that the slices are all equal
(usually, they cut it in the slicer).

Roll out your swordfish slices and cut them into four parts, with a spoon place the stuffing in the center of the slice, and close them in some way, perhaps helping with a toothpick. (If the rolls are not perfect, it does not matter, the important thing is that the stuffing does not come out).
Cut the large tomatoes into rounds and create a bed on the base of the slow cooker, place the roulades very gently on the tomatoes, pour the wine into the slow cooker and sprinkle the flour over the roulades.
Turn on the slow stove and cook for 4 hours on low.
Your delicious rolls are ready to be enjoyed!

Cod Balls

SERVE 4   PREPARATION 20m   COOKING 4h

INGREDIENTS

800g of clean cod
200g breadcrumbs
1 tablespoon olive oil
1 teaspoon freeze-dried garlic
1 broccoli
2 eggs
Chives
Salt and pepper to taste
Flour

INSTRUCTIONS

Take your cod fillets and with a fork break them up well going to remove all the bones. Be very careful not to leave any!
Then put the net cod meat into a blender with a little water and olive oil, and let it blend until it reduces to a mush.
Add your spices and breadcrumbs to the chopped cod and mix well. Form into small balls of about 150g each.
Dip the balls first in oil and then in flour and let them rest in the fridge for 30 minutes.
Cut the broccoli head into small pieces and form a bed with them on the bottom of the slow cooker, salt to taste and place the fish balls on top.
Turn on your slow stove and cook for 4 hours on bass mode.

Fish Skewers

SERVE 4   PREPARATION 20M   COOKING 4H

INGREDIENTS

Cod 300 gr
Salmon 300 g
Squid 200 g
Imperial prawns 10
Mixed peppers (yellow and red)
2 Courgettes
2 tablespoons extra virgin olive oil
100 ml fruity white wine
Mixed aromatic herbs (thyme, rosemary, basil,
parsley, or coriander)

INSTRUCTIONS

 The key to this recipe is a well-planned
preparation.
Clean the cod and salmon so that all scales and
bones are removed.
Then rinse the fish in cold water and cut cubes of
about 3 cm (it is very important that the size of the
cubes is uniform, so as to avoid that some pieces
cook less, or more, than others).
Clean the squid and cut them into equal parts and
cut the vegetables into equal parts.
At this point, take some long sticks and thread
your ingredients alternately in order to obtain
beautiful multi-colored skewers!
Create a thickness on the bottom of the slow
cooker using a special base that raises the skewers
2/3 centimeters.

Sprinkle your rolls evenly with the herbs and spices, then pour the wine over the bottom of the slow cooker, place the skewers in the centre (make sure they don't touch the base) and cook on low for about 4 minutes!
Wow, your succulent skewers are ready!
I personally like to serve this dish with a salad of cherry tomatoes and red onion.

Pesce spada alla Messinese

SERVE 4   PREPARATION 5m   COOKING 4.5h

INGREDIENTS

500g Swordfish
300g Cherry tomatoes
20 black olive groves
2 tablespoons extra virgin olive oil
1 clove Garlic
20 g Pine nuts
A few basil leaves
Salt and pepper to taste

INSTRUCTIONS

A really simple recipe to prepare and tasty!
Cut the cherry tomatoes in half or in 4, as you
prefer; make sure that the olives are without a
kernel (we don't want someone to break a tooth)
and cut them to half.
Then place olives, cherry tomatoes, chopped garlic,
and pine nuts at the base of the slow cooker
forming a bed , and pour a spoon of olive oil on top
of it.
When buying swordfish make sure your trusted
fishmonger cuts it by creating not too thin slices,
about 2/3 centimeters thick.
Place the slices of swordfish on the base you
created, pour in the wine, salt pepper and basil
leaves.
Switch on the slow cooker and cook for about 4.5
hours.

The dish is ready!
The perfect side dish to accompany the Messina swordfish and a green salad topped with oil and lemon.

Buon appetito!

Fish soup on slow cooker

SERVE 4   PREPARATION 1h   COOKING 4h

INGREDIENTS

8 red prawns
2 cuttlefish
500 g mussels
Toad tail
500 grams of grouper
2 tablespoons extra virgin olive oil
1 clove of chopped garlic
1 small glass of fruity rosé wine
Salt and pepper to taste
600 g tomato sauce
1 medium onion
2 celery stalks
2 carrots
Mix of aromatic herbs.

INSTRUCTIONS

Let's start by cleaning the whole fish. Remove head, tail, fins, central smooth, thorns, and skin (do not throw anything away).
All you must do is get some net fillets from your fish. I recommend being careful to eliminate all thorns (especially attention to mullet), it would be really unpleasant for one of your guests to find a herringbone in his mouth!
Put all the scraps obtained from your fish in a pot, add water until the whole thing is covered and bring to a boil, lower the heat and simmer for about half an hour. Filter everything with extreme care (use a strainer with exceedingly small meshes) and you have obtained the fish broth.
In a pan pour a spoon of extra virgin olive oil and a few drops of wine, heat well and add the mussels (make sure all mussels are closed), cook for a few minutes until the mussels all open. Shut down the fire and set it aside to cool.
Chop the onion, carrots and celery and place them inside the slow cooker with a drizzle of olive oil and start the slow cooker at low temperature, add the garlic and the rest of the wine.
Cook for 10 minutes (low mode) and add the fish fillets you had previously cleaned. Then take the mussels and add them to the soup (for space reasons you can remove the shells if you prefer).
Add the fish broth and after 10 minutes the tomato sauce and your herbs last.
Cook in low mode for about 4 hours.
Your delicious fish soup is ready! Serve it with croutons and you can rest assured to make a great impression on your guests!

Paper Mackerel

SERVE 4   PREPARATION 10m   COOKING 4h

INGREDIENTS

4 Whole mackerel
1 clove of garlic
2 celery stalks
2 red peppers
1 glass of dry white wine
100 g cherry tomatoes
1 eggplant
30 ml lemon juice
Some basil leaves
1 tablespoon extra virgin olive oil
Salt and pepper to taste
baking paper

INSTRUCTIONS

I personally recommend buying the mackerel
already cleaned by your trusted fishmonger,
If you cannot, clean them up.
Eliminate head, fins and central smooth. Swarm
them well under cold water.
Cut the vegetables finely and divide them into 4
equal parts.
Get a sheet of baking paper and cut it into 4 parts
about 20 cm each, so take your clean fish and
place them in the center of the pieces of paper (1
for each fish)
Chop the garlic, divide the 4 equal parts, then
place it inside the fish. Cover each fish with the
previously cut vegetables, add the lemon juice,
and close so that nothing comes out of the bag.

Create a base at the bottom of your slow cooker and place your fish rolled gently.
Cook for 4 hours in low mode and the dish is ready!

Neapolitan Grouper

SERVE 2   PREPARATION 10   COOKING 2h

INGREDIENTS

2 grouper fillets (about 250g each)
3 tablespoons extra virgin olive oil
1 onion
1 clove of garlic
salt and pepper to taste
15 capers in salt
1 glass of white wine
1 tablespoon chopped parsley
20 cherry tomatoes
10 black olives
Some bay leaf and sage

INSTRUCTIONS

Slide the cherry tomatoes in half and place them in the slow cooker. Place the 2 grouper fillets (make sure they are spine-free) on top of them then the rest of the ingredients. Close and cook for about 2 hours in low mode without opening the lid. The meat of the grouper is particularly soft, and does not need a long cooking, but be careful to not serve it raw!

Octopus Bolognese

SERVE 4   PREPARATION 10m   COOKING 4h

INGREDIENTS

1 whole octopus of about 1/2 kilo
250 g tomato sauce
1 small glass of fruity white wine
Mix vegetables (1 small carrot,1 onion,1 celery stalk)
1 clove of garlic
3 tablespoons olive oil
2 bay leaves
Salt and pepper to taste
Chopped parsley

INSTRUCTIONS

Ask your trusted fishmonger to clean the octopus for you.
Then cut it into small pieces and sauté them in a pan with a tablespoon of oil the diced vegetables, add the white wine and sauté for 10 minutes.
Transfer everything inside the slow cooker, add the tomato sauce, the chopped garlic the parsley the bay leaves, close the lid and let cook for 4 hours.

Vegetables

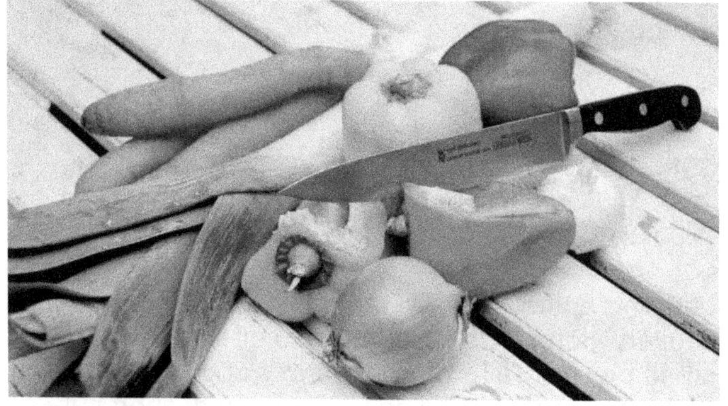

Hot Zucchini Salad

SERVE 4   PREPARATION 10m   COOKING 3h

INGREDIENTS

2 red peppers
4 zucchini
15 cherry tomatoes
Fresh chilly
1 tablespoon olive oil
1 onion
Chopped coriander
A few basil leaves
200g pecorino cheese (or parmesan cheese)
30g butter
Salt and pepper to taste

INSTRUCTIONS

Peel the onion, chop it and put it inside the slow
cooker, along with the zucchini cut into not too
small pieces. Take the peppers, sloppy them well
and remove the stem and all the seed, then cut
them into strips and put them in the slow cooker
as well. Add the butter, salt and black pepper and
cook in low mode. After about 1.5 hours add
chopped chili if you prefer, or you can also put it
whole so it can be easily removed if not welcome.
Then add the chopped coriander cheese and the
meta-cut poodles (or if you prefer the 4, but no
smaller than that) and a tablespoon of olive oil.
Cook for another hour and a half and the dish is
ready!
Garnish with fresh basil leaves

Grandma's Caponatina

SERVE 4　　　PREPARATION 10M　　　COOKING 3h

INGREDIENTS

2 Red peppers
2 aubergines
15 Capers
2 tablespoons pine nuts
1 White onion
2 tablespoons black olive groves
50 ml Extra virgin olive oil
500g tomato sauce
Some basil leaves
30 ml Balsamic vinegar
1 tsp Brown sugar
Salt and pepper to taste

INSTRUCTIONS

Cut the aubergines into not too small pieces, then take the peppers, remove the stem and seeds and slice them into small pieces, chop the onion and put everything inside the slow cooker.
Add all the ingredients and cook for 3 hours in low mode.
Grandma's Caponatina is ready!

Chickpea's soup

SERVE 4   PREPARATION 10   COOKING 5h

INGREDIENTS

1 kg Chickpeas
Some laurel leaves
1 celery stalk
 1 spoon of chopped parsley
1 onion
1 clove of garlic
10 cherry tomatoes
1 litre of homemade vegetable broth
1 teaspoon curry
Salt and pepper to taste

INSTRUCTIONS

In order to cook chickpeas and you need to leave
them submerged in water for 8/10 hours.

After this time the chickpeas softened and
therefore ready to be cooked.
Put them in the slow cooker together with the rest
of the ingredients and cook for 6 hours.
Remove the laurel leaves and blend everything (if
you prefer) with an immersion blender.
Your chickpea soup is ready!

Minestrone with Lentils

SERVE 8   PREPARATION 20m   COOKING 5h

INGREDIENTS

1 onion
2 carrots
3 celery stalks
3 tablespoons olive oil
500g dried lentils
100g peas
1 broccoli
2 cubes vegetable broth
1 liter of water
500g tomato sauce
Salt and black pepper to taste
Dry chilly to taste (optional)
Parmigiano to taste

INSTRUCTIONS

Chop the onions finely, then cut the carrots and celery into small cubes and put everything inside the slow cooker; add the lentils, olive oil and start the slow cooker in a high mode.
Have these vegetables cook for 30 minutes. In the meantime, put a liter of water to boil, where you will dissolve the stock cubes (stock cubes, it depends on the intensity of the variety you use, if they are intense enough only one, but usually I use 2 to enrich the minestrone), and leave it aside.
Pour the tomato sauce into the slow cooker and cook for another half-hour of high intensity. In total you will use the high mode for about 1 hour, then lower the intensity of the slow cooker.
Add the peas and broccoli cut into small pieces (try to use only the flowers and discard the stems) and cover everything with vegetable broth, black pepper and cook for another 4 hours in low mode. Your minestrone is ready!
Taste and correct salt if necessary (if you use 2 cubes of stock you can also avoid adding salt), and serve in a bowl with a sprinkle of parmesan on top.

Pasta with Beans

SERVE 8 PREPARATION 10m COOKING 6h

INGREDIENTS

500g bean mix
500g tomato sauce
1 onion
1 garlic clove
2 carrots
 2 celery stems
200g finely chopped cabbage
1 beef stock cube
1 liter of water
A few fresh basil leaves
1 kilo small pasta
Salt and pepper to taste
Parmesan to taste

INSTRUCTIONS

Before cooking the beans I highly recommend soaking them for 8 hours.
Chop the garlic and onion, and put them on the basis of the slow cooker, add the tomato together with the rest of the ingredients and cook for about 5/6 hours.
In a separate saucepan you will cook pasta. For pairing with beans I recommend using a type of small pasta such as orecchiette or dice, be very careful not to overcook it, indeed I recommend to take it out of the cooking water when it is still semi-cooked, because when you add it to the sauce with the beans it will continue to cook.
Then serve with a sprinkle of parmesan and your Pasta and Beans is ready!

Mediterranean asparagus

SERVES 8   PREPARATION 1m   COOKING 2h

INGREDIENTS

1 kilo of fresh asparagus
1 glass of lemon juice
1 glass of water
1 clove of garlic
Olive oil to taste
Salt and pepper to taste

INSTRUCTIONS

A healthy side dish very easy to prepare.
Put the asparagus inside the slow cooker. In a
separate container, mix the other ingredients
together and pour them over the asparagus.

Close the slow cooker and cook for 2 hours in low
mode.
Serve with a drizzle of olive oil.

Homemade tomato sauce

SERVE 8   PREPARATION 10m   COOKING 3

INGREDIENTS

20 ripe tomatoes
1/2 glass of water
Salt 2 teaspoons
Black pepper 2 teaspoons
A few basil leaves

INSTRUCTIONS

Rinse the tomatoes with cold water and make a
crosscut on the back that will serve to peel them
easily when cooked.
Put the tomatoes inside the slow cooker, add a
little water, close the lid and cook in medium mode
for 3 hours. At this point remove the skin from
each tomato and put them in a container, add salt
and black pepper (not obligatory) and blend
everything with an immersion blender. Add a few
basil leaves, stir and the sauce and ready to be
used in 1000 ways!

Pearl Barley soup

SERVE 4   PREPARATION 10M   COOKING 5h

INGREDIENTS

200 g pearl barley
1 carrot
1 onion
1 celery doll
2 potatoes
1 vegetable broth cube
Herbal mix (chives, thyme, dried basil)
2 tablespoons extra virgin olive oil
Salt and black pepper to taste
1 spoon of grated Parmesan cheese

INSTRUCTIONS

Finely chop celery, carrot and onion and sauté
them in a pan for a few minutes and transfer
everything to the slow cooker.
Add the pearl barley together with the spices and
start the slow cooker in low mode.
Separately boil a litre of water and melt inside the
cubes of vegetable stock.
Then pour everything into the slow cooker and
cook for 5 hours in low mode.
Serve with a sprinkle of Parmesan and herbal mix!

Spelt Soup

SERVE 4   PREPARATION 10m   COOKING   6h

INGREDIENTS

1 onion
2 carrots
2 zucchini
1 celery stalk
1 potato
300g Pearl spelled
200 grams of mixed beans
A few tablespoons of tomato sauce
Mixed herbs (Sage, Rosemary, Thyme)
1 veg stock cube
1 liter of water
3 tablespoon extra virgin olive oil
Salt and pepper to taste

INSTRUCTIONS

I recommend soaking both green beans and
spelled for an entire night before cooking them,
(no need if you use pearl spelled).
Cut the vegetables into little cubes and put them
inside the cooker sloe, add a few spoons of tomato
sauce.
Separately boil a liter of water and dissolve the
stock cube in it.
Pour the green beans and spelled, vegetable broth,
salt and pepper and your mixture of aromatic
herbs into your slow cooker.
Shut the lid and cook for 6 hours in low mode.
Serve with a spoonful of grated parmesan or
pecorino cheese.

Uncle Bill's Garden

SERVE 4   PREPARATION 10   COOKING 4h

INGREDIENTS

200g cabbage
200g spinach
1 broccoli
100g peas
1 onion
1 tuft of turnip tops
2 potatoes
1 veg stock cube
1 litre of water
2 tablespoons extra virgin olive oil
1/2 teaspoon lyophilized garlic
Fresh chilly
Salt and pepper to taste

INSTRUCTIONS

I think it's the simplest recipe ever invented!
Cut the vegetables into tiny pieces and put the
slow cooker inside. Boil the water and melt 1 or 2
cubes of veg stock (depending on what you use)
and pour the broth into the slow cooker along with
the vegetables.
Nail with the lid and cook for 4 hours at low
intensity.

Cereal soup

SERVE 4   PREPARATION 10M   COOKING 5H

INGREDIENTS

1 tablespoon extra virgin olive oil
2 liters vegetable broth
Vegetable mix (2 onions 1 carrot 1 potato)
200g dried peas
1 ladle of vegetable broth
300g barley
Salt and pepper to taste

INSTRUCTIONS

Chop the onions finely and put the slow cooker
inside together with the chopped carrot also finely
chopped. Remove the skin from the potatoes. Cut
it into tiny cubes and add it to the slow cooker.
Add a drizzle of olive oil, salt and pepper, dried
peas, barley and a ladle of vegetable broth.
Close the lid and cook for 5 hours in low mode.
The soup is ready

Pumpkin cream

SERVE 4   PREPARATIONS 10m   COOKING 3h

INGREDIENTS

600 g Pumpkin
300 g Fresh potatoes
1 onion
Fresh thyme(favourites herbs)
200 ml vegetable broth
3 tablespoons Extra virgin olive oil
Chopped coriander
Salt, black pepper and parmesan cheese to taste

INSTRUCTIONS

Cut your pumpkin into cubes after you clean it,
chop an onion and sauté it along with the diced
potatoes in a pan with olive oil.
Sauté for 10 minutes in the pan over medium heat
and transfer to the slow cooker.
Add the vegetable broth, herbs, salt and black
pepper, close the lid and cook for about 3 hours in
high mode.
After three hours then, blend everything and serve
it with a tablespoon of parmesan, dried chili
(optional) and a sprinkling of chopped coriander.
Good stick!
Ah, I forgot... you cannot help but dip croutons!

Cauliflower cream

SERVE 4　　　PREPARATION 10m　　COOKING 3h

INGREDIENTS

1 Whole cauliflower (about 800g)
The same amount of potatoes
2 leeks
1 onion
2 tablespoons extra virgin olive oil
1 clove of garlic
2 tablespoons butter
1 litre vegetable brood

INSTRUCTIONS

Clean the cauliflower head by pulling out only the soft and diced parts, then peel and dice the potatoes as well and finally the leeks with thin washers.
In a pan add the olive oil and heat well.
Put the vegetables into the pan and sauté for 10 minutes over medium heat, adding a chopped clove of garlic.
Put everything inside the slow cooker and add the butter and vegetable broth.
Close the lid and cook for 3 hours at high intensity.
Blend everything and serve!

Beef

SLOW BUFFALO SPICED

SERVE 2 PREPARATION 20 M   COOKING 8 H

INGREDIENTS

2 tablespoon extra-virgin olive oil
2 chipotle peppers in adobo sauce
300 ml grapefruit juice
1 lime, juiced
1 teaspoon fish sauce
2 big garlic cloves(or 3 small)
1/4 cup chopped fresh cilantro
1/2 teaspoon ground cumin
1/2 teaspoon paprika
Salt to taste
Any Steak you prefer, preferably with a medium fat
percentage

INSTRUCTIONS

-Prepare all the ingredients in the right amounts
(except the meat)and place them in the blender,
so start it and stir them until you obtain a soft
density;

-Take your steak (whatever cut you chose) and
give it a "sear" in a skillet over high heat on both
sides, don't let the meat cook for more than 20
seconds per side;
- Set your slow cooker to low and put in the meat
you seared earlier along with your centrifuged and
press start!
- Let your steaks absorb the flavor of the spices for
at least 8 hours ;

-After that, when the meat is deliciously tender, and you can easily cut it up and serve it on a bed of toasted bread or rocket salad.

Salsa Rollie

SERVE 4   PREPARATION 20   COOKING 6h

INGREDIENTS

8 slices of beef
15 slices of bacon, thinly sliced
300g of tomato sauce
1 garlic clove
1 onion
1 tablespoon of extra virgin olive oil
1 tablespoon Parmesan cheese
Coriander and fresh chilly to taste
Salt and pepper to taste

INSTRUCTIONS

Finely chop the garlic (you can also use freeze-
dried garlic) and mix it with the Parmesan cheese,
salt and pepper.
Lay the meat down and with a rolling pin or a
heavy spoon, hit it repeatedly in order to extend
the surface as much as possible.
After performing this process we should obtain thin
slices of meat that we will place well extended on a
plane. Then we are going to add a slice of bacon
and a teaspoon of the mixture of parmesan,
pepper, salt and garlic.
Roll the slice and close with a stick. Repeat the
process until you use all the ingredients.
Turn on the slow cooker and pour the sauce inside,
then plunge your rolls in and cook on low for 6
hours.

Slow Brisket with onion

SERVE 6   PREPARATION 25 m   COOKING 7h

INGREDIENTS

2 tablespoon extra virgin olive oil
2 large red onions cut in half
2 kilos beef brisket
6 cloves garlic, minced
2 cups low-sodium beef broth
2 tablespoons Worcestershire sauce
1 tablespoon soy sauce or tamari
Salt and ground black pepper to taste

INSTRUCTIONS

-Prepare a saucepan with a double bottom and
heat the oil well , then add the onions and brown
them for 15 minutes.
- Remove the onions from the pan and add the
meat , one piece at a time; let the meat pieces
sear on both sides.
-Place the pieces of meat in a 6-quart slow cooker
(place with the fat side not in contact with the
cooking surface) and add the minced garlic, the
previously cooked onions, the broth,
Worcestershire sauce and soy sauce or tamari.
-Cover and cook on low for at least 7 hours.

Slow Alabama Roast

SERVE 4   PREPARATION 15 m   COOKING 5 / 8 h

INGREDIENT

2 Kilos of boneless beef chuck roast
2 tablespoon extra virgin olive oil
½ kilo packet ranch salad dressing & seasoning
mix
600 g packet au jus gravy mix
200 g unsalted butter
2 kilos jar pepperoncini peppers
Salt and black pepper to taste

INSTRUCTIONS

-For this recipe is required a 6 litre slow cooker; if
you do not have one you can use a pot with a
capacity of more than 5 liters.

-Add the meat to the slow cooker (take care to bone it) then pour over all the seasonings and let it cook for at least 5 hours at medium temperature or 8 hours at low temperature (recommended).
-The meat should be ready if you have respected the cooking time, so taste it and correct it if you think it needs more salt or black pepper or maybe another half hour of cooking time.
At this point you can shred it and serve it with vegetables or a side salad.

Hunter roulades

SERVE 2 PREPARATION 10m COOKING 6h

INGREDIENTS

1/2 kilo of beef slices
100 g of thinly sliced bacon
1g of tomato sauce
2 tablespoon of extra virgin olive oil
Parmesan cheese
100g pitted black olives
50g capers
coriander
garlic
onion
salt and pepper to taste

INSTRUCTIONS

Prepare a large work surface to work neatly, then place the slices of meat on a plane, open them and season with a slice of bacon, parmesan and parsley, roll them and close them with a toothpick, make them open.
Separately we will prepare our sauce by frying with extra virgin olive oil a whole clove of garlic with coarsely chopped onion, olives, capers and coriander.
Sauté for 10 minutes over medium heat, constantly stirring to avoid sticking to the pan, then transfer to the slow cooker and place the rolls on top.
Let the slow cooker run for 6 hours at slow intensity and enjoy!

Buffalo spiced ribs

SERVE 4   PREPARATION 20m   COOKING 7h

INGREDIENTS

800g beef short ribs
the mixture of spices with a prevalence of garlic
black pepper and salt to taste
a splash of olive oil

INSTRUCTIONS

We prepare our short ribs for long cooking by removing the outer part of the fat leaving only a light layer to cover the meat.
At this point that we have clean chops, wet your hands with olive oil and massage the meat in order to create a light layer of olive oil and sprinkle the chops with our favorite spice mix, be careful not to leave any empty space but at the same time do not overdo it with spices, especially with salt.
We are going to arrange our chops in the center of the slow cooker and avoid that the part with the meat is in contact with the base.
Set the slow stove to low mode and let it cook for 7 hours.
At this point the ribs will be deliciously flavorful and juicy, ready to be served with mashed potatoes.

Classic Italian braised beef

SERVE 4   PREPARATIONS 10m   COOKING 6h

INGREDIENTS

800g shoulder or roast beef
2 tablespoons olive oil
200g porcini mushrooms
2 stalks of celery, chopped
500g tomato sauce
2 onions (not too big)
3 carrots
1 teaspoon of lyophilized garlic
300 ml full-bodied red wine
Salt and pepper to taste

INSTRUCTIONS

Turn on the oven to 200g and let it heat for about
10 minutes.
Prepare a tray with some baking paper, lay the
beef on it, and cook it for 10 minutes so as to get a
light browning.
In a frying pan, sauté the vegetables and spices for
10 minutes, then add the tomato sauce, wine and
bring to a boil, then lower the heat to a simmer,
pour everything into the slow cooker, place the
meat on top of the vegetables and cook on low for
at least 6 hours.
Your stew is ready!
In Sicily, it is very common to accompany the stew
with bread, while in the north they prefer polenta.

Beef Listrelle

SERVE 4   PREPARATION 5m   COOKING 4h

INGREDIENTS

4 Sirloin beef steaks
4 tablespoons olive oil
3 onions
2 tablespoons freeze-dried garlic
1 handful of flour
500 ml full-bodied red wine
4 sage leaves
1 cube of beef stock
1 tablespoon of tomato sauce
Salt and pepper to taste

INSTRUCTIONS

Take the steaks, cut them into strips and sprinkle them evenly with flour and set them aside.
Chop the onion very finely and sauté in a pan with the rest of the ingredients (except the meat and flour) for 10 minutes over low heat, then add the floured steak strips and cook and mix for another 10 minutes over medium heat.
Transfer to your slow stove and cook at medium intensity for at least 4 hours.

Beef shreds

SERVE 4   PREPARATION 10m   COOKING 5/6 h

INGREDIENTS

4 sirloin steaks (or any other beef steak that is not
overly fatty)
500 of tomato sauce
2 small onions
1 garlic clove
1 tablespoon olive oil
rosemary, white pepper, coriander and sage to
taste
150 ml full-bodied red wine (or whatever you have
open at home)
1 cube of beef stock
salt to taste

INSTRUCTIONS

I personally recommend marinating the meat
before cooking it so you can achieve an explosion
of flavours!
Cut the meat into tiny shreds and place it in an
airtight bag along with the rest of the ingredients.
Leave overnight to marinate, but do not exceed 12
hours.
Open your airtight bag and pour the contents into
the slow cooker.
Set the temperature to low and cook for 5 to 6
hours.
This dish goes very well with polenta.

The original Goulash

SERVE 4   PREPARATION 10m   COOKING 8h

INGREDIENTS

1kg beef stew
2 red peppers
2 potatoes
2 onion
2 big carrot
750g tomato sauce
2 teaspoons of freeze-dried paprika and cumin
1 tablespoon olive oil
Salt and pepper to taste

INSTRUCTIONS

Finely cut the onion, and fry it with extra virgin olive oil, add the vegetables cut into small pieces and fry for a few minutes.
Transfer the contents to the slow stove, add the meat and spices and cook on low for 8 hours!

Simple and delicious, this is a typical dish of Hungarian culture; how not to accompany this dish with bread?

Beef in beer

SERVE 4   PREPARATION 10m   COOKING 5h

INGREDIENTS

4 lean beef steaks
1 amber beer of 500 ml
1 spoon extra virgin olive oil
Veggie mix (celery, carrots, and onion)
Salt and pepper to taste

INSTRUCTIONS

Take your steaks and cut them into shreds, then place them inside an airtight bag and cover them with beer.
Place the bag inside the fridge and let it marinate overnight.
Very important not to put salt during the marinating with beer.
Chop the vegetables into small pieces and fry them for 5 minutes with a tablespoon of olive oil.
Pour the vegetables into the slow cooker.
Open the bag and take out the marinated meat, add it to the greens inside the slow cooker with about 200 ml of the beer you used for marinating and let the slow cooker run for 5 hours on pass mode.
Taste and add salt pepper or spices to taste.
The dish goes well with sautéed broccoli with butter and peas.

Porto beef stew

SERVE 4   PREPARATION 10M   COOKING   6H

INGREDIENTS

4 beefsteak from about 200g each with little fat
1 tablespoon olive oil
100ml ruby port
200g porcini mushrooms
100g pine nuts
100g walnuts
1 onion
1 teaspoon lyophilized garlic
50g white flour
Salt and black pepper and Thyme to taste

INSTRUCTIONS

Chop the onions and sauté them with olive oil
along with the mushrooms. Cut the steaks into
small cubes and add them to the pan, raise the
heat and add the pot, bring to a boil, remove from
the heat and pour inside the slow cooker.
Add the garlic, dried fruit and turn on the slow
cooker; cook for about 6 hours in low mode. After
that, add the spices and a sprinkle of flour and mix
well.
Ready and Delicious!

Chicken

Entire Rosemary Juicy Chicken

SERVE 2   PREPARATION 5 m COOKING 3 to 5 h

INGREDIENTS

- 1 whole chicken
- Salt and pepper to taste
- Fresh rosemary
- 1 whole lemon

INSTRUCTIONS

As a base for cooking our chicken, we will lay a metal base on the bottom of the slow cooker (you can use a wire rack or something similar if you really don't have any object that will fit use tin foil rolled up to form 3 balls, but don't put the chicken directly in contact with the bottom of the slow cooker)

-Clean the chicken inside by removing the internal organs and dry it well with paper before placing it for cooking.
-Season the chicken with salt and pepper and add it to the slow cooker along with some twigs of rosemary and a lemon cut in 4 pieces.
-Very important when placing the chicken in the slow cooker, make sure that the breast side is facing upwards and that it remains in the center during cooking which will obviously take place over very low heat (set the lowest temperature available on your slow cooker) and cook for at least 3 hours (it is not possible to determine a precise cooking time as the chickens may be of different sizes but it is advisable to check internally that the chicken is cooked enough before serving).

Chicken Sud Italia

SERVE 4   PREPARATION 25m   COOKING 3h

INGREDIENTS

Ingredients
4 chicken thighs
50g of butter
2 glasses of dry white wine
50 ml of white wine vinegar
2 garlic cloves
1 onion
3 sprigs of rosemary
2 tablespoons of extra virgin olive oil
200 pitted white olives
Chopped coriander
Salt and black pepper to taste

INSTRUCTIONS

To prepare this delicious dish, it is necessary to act one day in advance, as the chicken meat will be marinated for at least 12 hours.

Marinating

Prepare a container with a lid in which you will pour the wine, vinegar, garlic, rosemary, a teaspoon of salt, and the chicken thighs, stir carefully and make sure that all the meat is wet from the liquid. Shut the container and leave it in the refrigerator for at least 12 hours (it does not hurt a few more hours); it would be ideal for turning the thighs after 6 hours in order to immerse the part that was dry.

Cooking

Remove the chicken from the container in which you left it to marinate and dry the meat well with paper towels and set aside.
Sauté the onion with olive oil, add the olives, more rosemary, a whole clove of garlic (to give it a more delicate flavor) which you will then remove and let it brown over low heat for less than 10 minutes. Place the chicken thighs in the slow cooker and pour the sauté over the chicken along with 30 ml white wine, butter and chopped coriander salt and black pepper and leave to cook over medium heat for no less than 3 hours.
At this point the dish is ready. You can serve the chicken thighs with a side of broccoli.

Chicken Pork Wedding

SERVE 4 PREPARATION 10 M   COOKING 5 H

INGREDIENTS

3 kilos thick-cut bacon, diced
small fennel bulb, bulb diced
2 diced yellow onion
8 cloves garlic, minced
tablespoons all-purpose flour
2 tablespoon extra virgin olive oil
1 glass fruity white wine
1 kilo boneless, skinless chicken thighs, all of them
cut in half
1 1/4 cups low-sodium chicken broth
300 grams tomato sauce
Salt and Black pepper to taste

INSTRUCTIONS

-Start cooking the bacon over medium heat for
several minutes so that it becomes crispy and
releases the fat that we will remove, leaving just a
small amount of it;

- Add some olive oil, garlic cut not too fine, onion
and fennel with a little salt and pepper and cook
for at least 5 minutes over low heat.

-Put the chicken, broth, tomato and the vegetables
you cooked earlier into your slow cooker, set it low
modality and let it cook for about 5 hours.

-At this point the meat should be soft enough to pull away from the bones, so place the boneless meat back in the pot, taste and correct it and if you think it needs more salt or black pepper or maybe another half hour of cooking.

-If you think it is ready serve on a bed of mashed potato or roasted potatoes or any grilled vegetables you like.

Slow Citrusy Chicken Breast

SERVE 4   PREPARATION 25 m COOKING 3 to 4 h

INGREDIENTS

- 2 tablespoon olive oil
- 4 medium chicken breasts
- 1 cup low-sodium chicken broth
- Juice of 3 lime
- 8 cloves garlic, smashed
- 200g butter
- 300g flour
- Salt and black pepper to taste
- Pinch of fresh chilly and oregano
- Chopped coriander

INSTRUCTIONS

-Cook the chicken on its own first, with a little oil.
Brown both sides for at least 5 minutes until
golden brown.
-Transfer the chicken to your 6 litre slow cooker (if
you don't have such a big one, you can use a pot
with a lid). Add the lime juice and garlic and let it
cook at medium temperature for at least 3 to 4
hours.
-Separately, mix the flour and butter in a bowl.
-Now you can plate the chicken, transfer the liquid
with which it was cooked to a pan where you are
going to add your mixture of flour and butter and
stir slowly, cooking over low heat until everything
is perfectly mixed and pour it over the chicken.
-Finish the dish with coriander chopped on top

The perfect side dish to go with it is stimmed broccoli with grated parmesan on top.

Shanghai Chicken

SERVE 4   PREPARATION 30M   COOKING 4H

INGREDIENTS

6 small or 4 medium chicken thighs
1 tablespoon olive oil
5 dates
50 g shelled and chopped almonds
fresh chili pepper
50g of honey
30 ml water
3 dried figs
the special mixture of spices
(chopped rosemary, garlic powder, white pepper
powder, salt to taste).

INSTRUCTIONS

Let's marinate the chicken thighs first.
Honey and chili sauce:
Take the honey and transfer it into a glass jar (if
not already), close it well and immerse it in hot
water in order to make the honey almost liquid.
In the meantime, take the fresh chili, chop it and
boil it with 50 ml of water in a small saucepan for
few minutes and pour it into a small container,
where you will combine it with the honey (if almost
all the water evaporated, add a little more until
you reach 50 ml again).
Mix well and sprinkle the chicken thighs with this
honey and chili sauce, massage well to cover the
entire surface.

Take the spice mix you prepared earlier and pour it over the chicken thighs so as to cover them all evenly.
Put the thighs in the refrigerator and let them marinate overnight.

Cooking:

We take our marinated thighs and place them inside the slow cooker, pour over the dates, chopped almonds and figs, and put them together with a tablespoon of olive oil and set the slow cooker for 4 hours on low mode.

Peanut Chicken

SERVE 4   PREPARATION 15m   COOKING 5 h

INGREDIENTS

8 chicken thighs
1/2kg ground peanuts
8 tablespoons olive oil
3 white onions
2 garlic cloves
1 tablespoon of cumin
150g of tomato sauce
A pinch of paprika
1 tablespoon of Aji Amarillo
Salt and pepper to taste

INSTRUCTIONS

Start by crushing the peanuts with a rolling pin or any heavy object after putting them in a bag. Make sure they are reduced to small pieces.
Take a large frying pan and sauté the onion (finely chopped) in olive oil along with tomato sauce and all the other ingredients. Sauté over low heat for 10 minutes.
Turn on the slow stove, pour the contents of the pan inside and let it cook for 5 hours on medium mode.
The dish is ready!
It pairs perfectly with a side of sweet potatoes.

Coxas de frango brasileiras

SERVE 4   PREPARATION 20m   COOKIN 4h

INGREDIENTS

8 chicken thighs
200 g cashews
2 garlic cloves
1/2 kg of tomato sauce
1 medium onion
300g single cream
1 tablespoon of spicy Indian curry
1/2 tablespoon of white pepper
Salt to taste

INSTRUCTIONS

First of all, I suggest breaking the peanuts into small pieces. You can proceed in different ways, for example, placing the peanuts inside a bag or a piece of cloth and hitting them repeatedly with a rolling pin.
Heat a thick-bottomed roasting pan, take the chicken thighs, and cook them for 5 minutes per side.
Chop the onion and sauté with the rest of the ingredients for 10 minutes, then pour into the slow cooker and add the chicken thighs on top.
Set the slow stove to medium mode and let it cook for about 4 hours.
Your chicken thighs are ready to be eaten!
You can serve them with fries.

Macedonia Chicken

SERVE 4   PREPARATION 10m   COOKING 5h

INGREDIENTS

4 large chicken thighs
30 ml of white wine vinegar
30 ml water
1 garlic clove
2 sprigs of rosemary
4 basil leaves
2 tablespoon olive oil
Salt and pepper to taste

INSTRUCTIONS

for an excellent result of this dish is necessary a marinating of at least 12 hours.
Then take an airtight food bag and place the chicken thighs inside.
Cut the garlic into 4 parts and add it to the marinade along with the vinegar and rosemary.
Leave to marinate overnight, but no longer than 12 hours.
Pour the water into the slow cooker and remove the chicken from the bag.
Set to low mode and cook for 6 hours.

Stuffed Whole Chicken

SERVE 4   PREPARATION 30m   COOKING 5h

INGREDIENTS

1 whole chicken
200g bacon
100g cheddar
150g cooked ham
1 egg
100g breadcrumbs
100ml olive oil
Salt, black pepper, barbeque spices mix to taste.

INSTRUCTIONS

Take a whole chicken and remove any unwanted
parts, such as internal organs, feathers, or bones,
and place inside an airtight food bag along with the
spice mixture and olive oil. Leave the chicken to
marinate overnight in the fridge.
Create the stuffing with the rest of the ingredients
until it forms a sort of paste.
Then take the chicken and stuff it with the mixture
and close it with some string in order to keep the
stuffing inside.
Create a base on the bottom of the slow cooker to
hold the chicken up at least 2/3 inches.
Start the slow stove on low mode and cook for 6
hours.
The dish is ready! Enjoy a side of fried vegetables.

Chicken pate

SERVE 4   PREPARATION 10   COOKING 6h

INGREDIENTS

200 g of internal organs (liver or heart or lungs)
80ml brandy (the cheapest one you have at home)
Vinegar
2 tablespoons olive oil
100 g butter
1 onion
1 carrot
1 celery stick
2 tomatoes
1 clove of garlic
2 bay leaves
200 ml broth
Salt and black pepper to taste

INSTRUCTIONS

Put the entrails to marinate in an airtight bag with vinegar for 2 hours.
Prepare a pot where you will sauté with olive oil and onion finely chopped together with the carrot, tomatoes, and celery, also finely chopped.
Add the entrails to the sauté and let cook for 5 minutes over low heat.
Pour your sauté into the slow cooker, add a coarsely cut clove of garlic and the rest of the ingredients.
Let cook for 5 hours over low heat.
Taste and if you think the meat need another hour of cooking, let go of another hour.
Pour the contents into a baking tray and let cool.
Remove the bay leaves and when it is cold enough, blend everything.
Your chicken pate is ready to be enjoyed on toasted pieces of bread!

Chicken curry

SERVES 2   PREPARATION 10M   COOKING 3H

INGREDIENTS

1/2 Chicken breast (about 400 g)
200ml coconut milk
1 spoon olive oil
100g of pineapple
1 onion
1 tablespoon curry
Salt and white pepper to taste

INSTRUCTIONS

Cut the chicken into not too small cubes and sauté for a few minutes with a thinly chopped onion and a tablespoon of olive oil. Transfer everything inside the slow cooker, add the coconut milk, curry and pineapple cut into cubes and cook high for at least 3 hours.
After that taste and adjust salt and white pepper.
Serve with sticky rice!

Chicken Chardonnay

SERVE 4   PREPARATION 10   COOKING 3h

INGREDIENTS

1 Whole chicken breast (about 800g)
2 tablespoons of extra virgin olive oil
Mixed herbs (basil leaves, sage and thyme)
1 tablespoon lyophilized garlic
The juice of a ripe lemon
125 ml Chardonnay
1 tablespoon Flour
Salt and white pepper to taste
40ml chicken stock

INSTRUCTIONS

Cut the chicken breast into little cubes of about one centimetre and put them in a pan with a tablespoon of olive oil. Raise the heat and add the wine and lemon juice cook for a few minutes and transfer to the slow cooker.
Add the flour, garlic, herbs, chicken broth, salt and white pepper, close the lid and cook for 3 hours at high mode.
And ready!
Serve with a lettuce and cucumber salad and of course a chilled bottle of Chardonnay!